PEYTON MANNING, LENNY MOORE, ALAN AMECHE, MARVIN HARRISON, RAYMOND BERRY, JOHN MACKEY, BOB VOGEL, TARIK GLENN, JIM PARKER, CHRIS HINTON, RAY DONALDSON, GINO MA[illegible] DWIGHT FREENEY, ART DONO[illegible] LIPSCOMB, DON SHINNICK, MIKE CURTIS, TED HENDRICKS, LENNY LYLES, BRUCE LAIRD, JERRY LOGAN, BOB SANDERS, MIKE VANDERJAGT, ROHN STARK,

PEYTON MANNING, LENNY MOORE, ALAN AMECHE, MARVIN HARRISON, RAYMOND BERRY, JOHN MACKEY, BOB VOGEL, TARIK GLENN, JIM PARKER, CHRIS HINTON,

THE STORY OF THE INDIANAPOLIS COLTS

COLTS
85
35 SEASONS
85

THE STORY OF THE INDIANAPOLIS COLTS

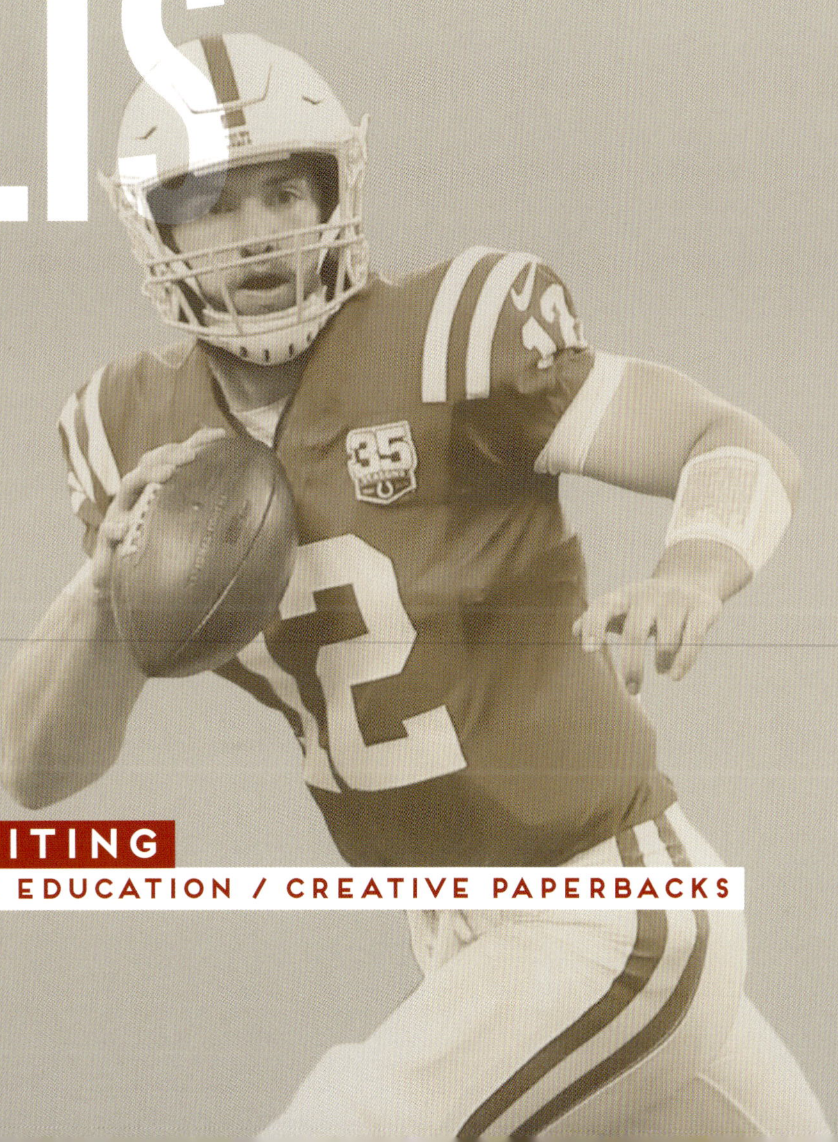

BY JIM WHITING

CREATIVE EDUCATION / CREATIVE PAPERBACKS

PUBLISHED BY CREATIVE EDUCATION AND CREATIVE PAPERBACKS
P.O. BOX 227, MANKATO, MINNESOTA 56002
CREATIVE EDUCATION AND CREATIVE PAPERBACKS ARE IMPRINTS OF THE CREATIVE COMPANY
WWW.THECREATIVECOMPANY.US

DESIGN AND PRODUCTION BY BLUE DESIGN (WWW.BLUEDES.COM)
ART DIRECTION BY RITA MARSHALL
PRINTED IN CHINA

PHOTOGRAPHS BY AP IMAGES (AP, ASSOCIATED PRESS), CORBIS (BETTMANN), GETTY IMAGES (VERNON BIEVER, DIAMOND IMAGES, FOCUS ON SPORT, CHRIS GRAYTHEN, JEFF GROSS, JEFF HAYNES/AFP, MICHAEL HICKEY/STRINGER, KIDWILER COLLECTION/DIAMOND IMAGES, STREETER LECKA, NEIL LEIFER/SI, ANDY LYONS, BRAD MANGIN/SI, DONALD MIRALLE, NFL, DARRYL NORENBERG/NFL, STACY REVERE, ROBERT RIGER, FRANK RIPPON/NFL, OWEN C. SHAW, JOHN SLEEZER/KANSAS CITY STAR/MCT, RICK STEWART/ALLSPORT)

NAMES: WHITING, JIM, AUTHOR.
TITLE: THE STORY OF THE INDIANAPOLIS COLTS / JIM WHITING.
SERIES: NFL TODAY.
INCLUDES INDEX.
SUMMARY: THIS HIGH-INTEREST HISTORY OF THE NATIONAL FOOTBALL LEAGUE'S INDIANAPOLIS COLTS HIGHLIGHTS MEMORABLE GAMES, SUMMARIZES SEASONAL TRIUMPHS AND DEFEATS, AND FEATURES STANDOUT PLAYERS SUCH AS PEYTON MANNING.
IDENTIFIERS: LCCN 2018041020 / ISBN 978-1-64026-143-3 (HARDCOVER) / ISBN 978-1-62832-706-9 (PBK) / ISBN 978-1-64000-261-6 (EBOOK)
SUBJECTS: LCSH: INDIANAPOLIS COLTS (FOOTBALL TEAM)—HISTORY—JUVENILE LITERATURE. / BALTIMORE COLTS (FOOTBALL TEAM)—HISTORY—JUVENILE LITERATURE.
CLASSIFICATION: LCC GV956.153 W44 2019 / DDC 796.332/640977252—DC23

FIRST EDITION HC 9 8 7 6 5 4 3 2 1
FIRST EDITION PBK 9 8 7 6 5 4 3 2 1

COVER: ANDREW LUCK
PAGE 2: ERIC EBRON
PAGES 6–7: DARIUS BUTLER

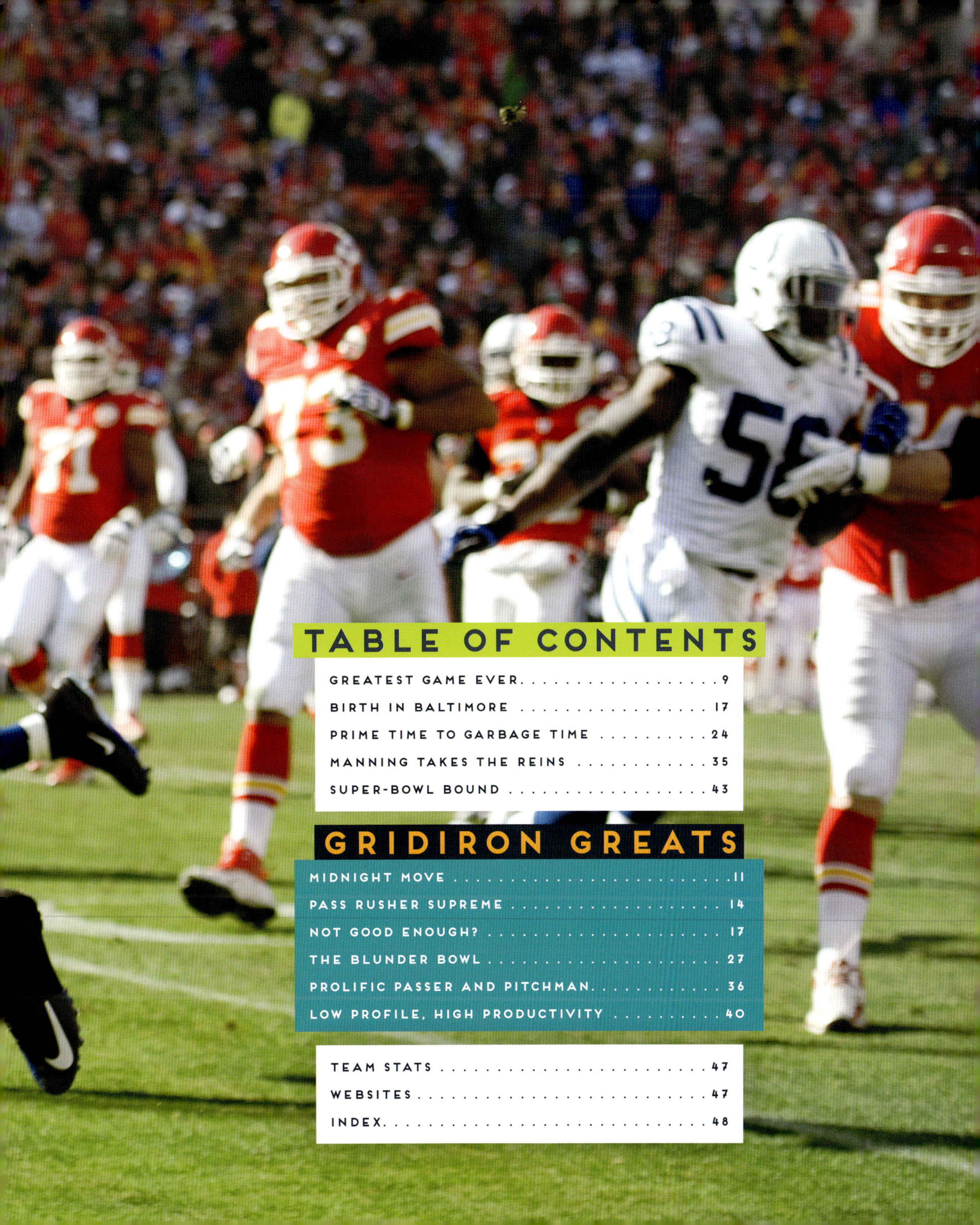

TABLE OF CONTENTS

GRIDIRON GREATS

LONGINES
GIANTS
0
VISITORS
0
QUARTER
1
DOWN
2
PLAY BY
YDS. TO GO
BALL ON 29 YD LINE
8
42
42
33
62

GREATEST GAME EVER

In 1958, professional football was still not a very popular sport. Many sports fans considered it something to fill the gap between the end of Major League Baseball season and the start of spring training. More people watched horse racing than National Football League (NFL) games. But in 1958, CBS decided to televise the championship game. It would be shown nationwide. The New York Giants hosted the game. They had been in the NFL for more than 30 years. They already had four NFL titles. The Baltimore Colts were fairly new to the league. They had joined in 1953. This was just their second winning season.

Baltimore took an early 14–3 lead. But the Giants stormed back. New York led by three points late in the fourth quarter. Less than two minutes remained in the game. The Colts had no timeouts. "When we got in the huddle," said end Raymond Berry, "I looked down the field, and the goal posts looked like they were in Baltimore." Quarterback Johnny Unitas and Berry connected three times. Just seven seconds were left. Steve Myhra trotted onto the field to attempt a game-tying field goal. He had missed more than half of his field goals during the season. The Giants had blocked his 27-yard attempt in the first quarter. "I told myself I better not miss it, or it would be a long, cold winter back on the farm in North Dakota," Myhra said. He didn't miss.

For the first time in league history, the championship game went into overtime. The Giants won the coin toss. But they couldn't score. The ball went to the Colts. They reached the Giants' 1-yard line. Unitas called "16 power." Blockers opened a gaping hole in the line. Hard-charging fullback Alan "The Horse" Ameche wrapped both hands around the ball. He lowered his head. Then he plowed into the end zone. The photo of him crossing the goal line is one of most famous in NFL history. "It was probably the shortest

LEFT: 1958 NFL CHAMPIONSHIP

BALTIMORE, MARYLAND
MARCH 28–29, 1984

GRIDIRON GREATS
MIDNIGHT MOVE

During the late 1970s and early 1980s, the Colts suffered several losing seasons. Fan attendance was low. The once-proud franchise hoped for a new stadium. But owner Robert Irsay (pictured) couldn't convince the city to fund it. He threatened to move the team. On March 28, 1984, the state of Maryland passed an eminent domain law. It could have allowed the city to claim ownership of the team. Irsay was afraid that his franchise was in danger. He quickly decided to move the Colts to Indianapolis. That very night, all team property was loaded into moving trucks. When Baltimore fans awoke the next morning, their team was gone.

ALAN AMECHE

"IT WAS PROBABLY THE SHORTEST RUN I EVER MADE AND THE MOST REMEMBERED."

—ALAN "THE HORSE" AMECHE

run I ever made and the most remembered," said Ameche. It seemed fitting that "The Horse" scored the winning touchdown in the Colts' first-ever championship game.

The contest quickly became known as the "Greatest Game Ever Played." It likely led to the NFL's rise in popularity. "If you were going to point to one game that gave the NFL momentum..., it would have to be the 1958 championship game," said NFL commissioner Pete Rozelle. "It gave us a tremendous boost with television." Colts defensive tackle Art Donovan added, "Everybody started getting interested in the game. I think that was the start of something big." Soon, football began to challenge baseball as the country's national pastime.

GINO MARCHETTI
DEFENSIVE END

COLTS SEASONS: 1953–64, 1966
HEIGHT: 6-FOOT-4
WEIGHT: 244 POUNDS

GRIDIRON GREATS
PASS RUSHER SUPREME

The last thing a quarterback wanted to see was Gino Marchetti staring at him across the line of scrimmage. For more than a decade, Marchetti was one of the NFL's most feared pass rushers. Before that, he was a machine gunner in World War II. He fought in the Battle of the Bulge. Marchetti was a great all-around defensive end. He was at his best in passing situations. He was known as a violent, yet clean, hitter. Many teams double- or even triple-teamed him to protect their passer. That strategy only opened more opportunities for Marchetti's teammates.

11

11 PRO BOWLS IN 14 YEARS

161

161 GAMES PLAYED

LINEBACKER ALEX AGASE (NUMBER 62) AND DEFENSIVE HALFBACK BERT RECHICHAR

BIRTH IN BALTIMORE

In 1947, a group of businessmen purchased the Miami Seahawks. The Seahawks were a failing team from the All-America Football Conference (AAFC). The new owners asked fans to rename the franchise. Charles Evans, a Maryland native, suggested Colts. It reflected Baltimore's proud horse racing tradition. The Preakness Stakes is the second leg of the sport's Triple Crown. The race is held in Baltimore each May.

The AAFC merged with the NFL in 1950. The Colts

posted a miserable 1–11 record. The league dissolved the team due to financial problems. Then, in December 1952, NFL commissioner Bert Bell laid down a challenge. Baltimore could have an NFL team if the city sold 15,000 season tickets in six weeks. Fans easily reached that quota. The Colts were back!

During their first three seasons, the Colts went a combined 11–24–1. They had a few talented players. Tackle Art Donovan and end Gino Marchetti anchored the defense. But the team lacked an on-field leader. Johnny Unitas showed up at training camp before the 1956 season. He was hoping for a tryout. He got one. He became the leader the team needed. Unitas led the Colts to a 7–5 record in 1957. In 1958, they jumped to 9–3. By then, the team's high-powered offense featured more stars. Ameche, Berry, and sure-handed halfback Lenny Moore were on the running and receiving end of the ball. According to *Sports Illustrated*, Berry had "a bad back and one leg shorter than the other so that he wears mud cleats on that shoe to equalize them. His eyes are so bad that he must wear contact lenses when he plays." Still, he played a key role in the Colts' memorable win over the Giants. He would go on to set NFL career receiving records.

The Colts met the Giants in the championship game again the following year. Unitas sparked the Colts. They scored 24 points in the fourth quarter. Baltimore won, 31–16. That performance solidified the legend of "Johnny U." "You can't intimidate him," said Los Angeles Rams defensive tackle Merlin Olsen. "When he sees us coming,

COACH WEEB EWBANK

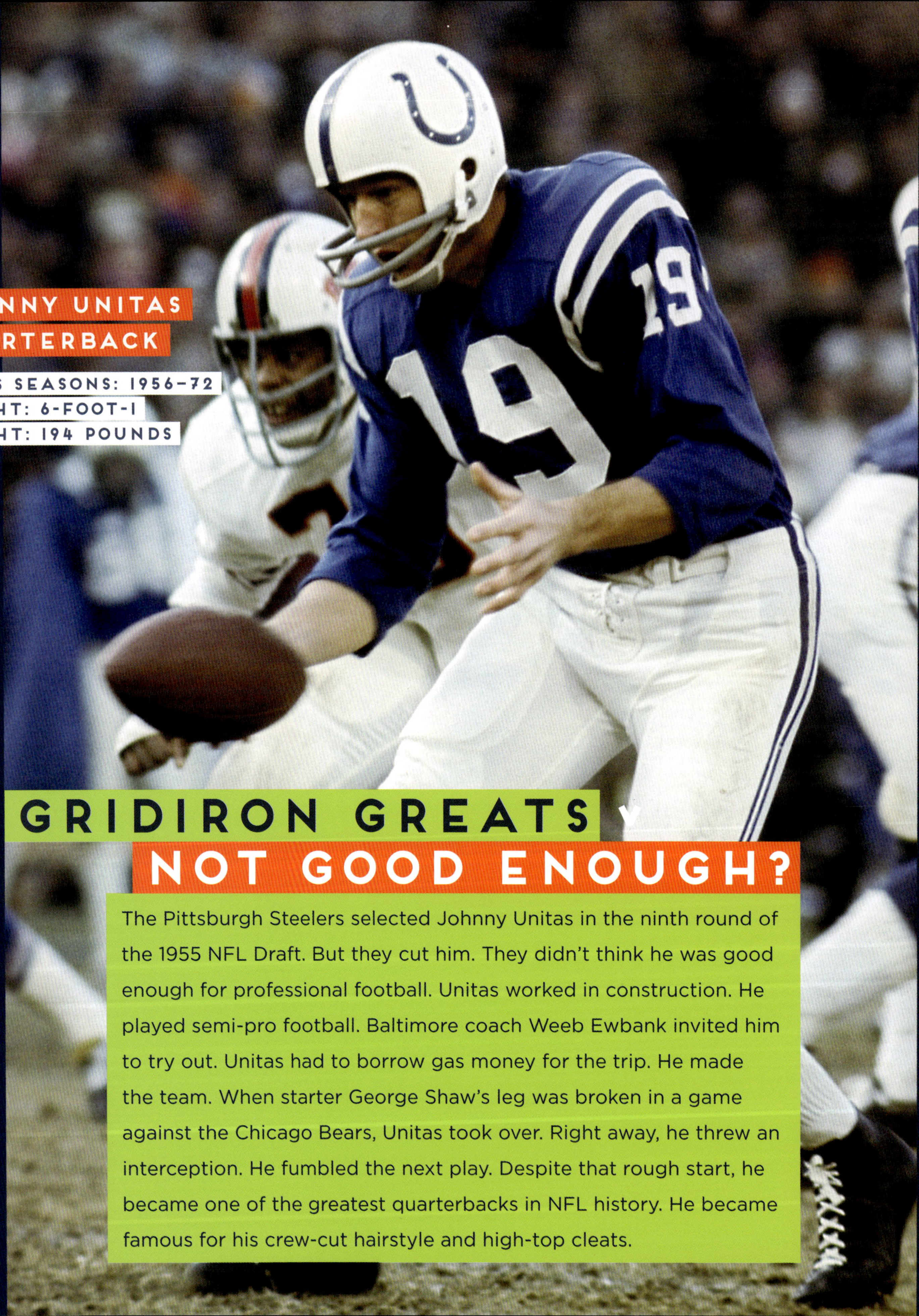

JOHNNY UNITAS
QUARTERBACK

COLTS SEASONS: 1956–72
HEIGHT: 6-FOOT-1
WEIGHT: 194 POUNDS

GRIDIRON GREATS

NOT GOOD ENOUGH?

The Pittsburgh Steelers selected Johnny Unitas in the ninth round of the 1955 NFL Draft. But they cut him. They didn't think he was good enough for professional football. Unitas worked in construction. He played semi-pro football. Baltimore coach Weeb Ewbank invited him to try out. Unitas had to borrow gas money for the trip. He made the team. When starter George Shaw's leg was broken in a game against the Chicago Bears, Unitas took over. Right away, he threw an interception. He fumbled the next play. Despite that rough start, he became one of the greatest quarterbacks in NFL history. He became famous for his crew-cut hairstyle and high-top cleats.

211

211 GAMES PLAYED

290

290 CAREER PASSING TOUCHDOWNS

"WHEN HE SEES US COMING, HE KNOWS IT'S GOING TO HURT, AND WE KNOW IT'S GOING TO HURT. BUT HE JUST STANDS THERE AND TAKES IT."

—MERLIN OLSEN ON JOHNNY UNITAS

he knows it's going to hurt, and we know it's going to hurt. But he just stands there and takes it."

The Colts struggled during the early 1960s. Then they acquired talented players such as tight end John Mackey. The team had an 11-game winning streak in 1964. It finished the season with 12 wins. This put the Colts back in the NFL Championship Game. But they were swamped by the Cleveland Browns, 27–0. The Colts made the playoffs in 1965. The Green Bay Packers beat them in overtime. The Colts made a bit of odd history in 1967. They went 11–1–2. The lone loss was in the final game against the Rams. That created a tie for the Coastal Division title. Los Angeles held the tiebreaker. Baltimore missed the playoffs.

JOHN MACKEY

PRIME TIME TO GARBAGE TIME

The Colts overcame their disappointment in 1968. They galloped to a 13–1 record. They smashed the Browns, 34–0, to advance to Super Bowl III. They were favored to win. Their opponent was the New York Jets. The Jets represented the American Football League (AFL). New York's quarterback was "Broadway Joe" Namath. He boldly predicted that his team would win. People laughed. The NFL's Packers had easily won the first two Super Bowls. This seemed to show that the NFL was far superior to the AFL. But Broadway Joe was right. He led the Jets to a 16–7 win. This proved that AFL teams could compete with the NFL.

JOHNNY UNITAS

11

11 COMBINED TURNOVERS

14

14 COMBINED PENALTIES

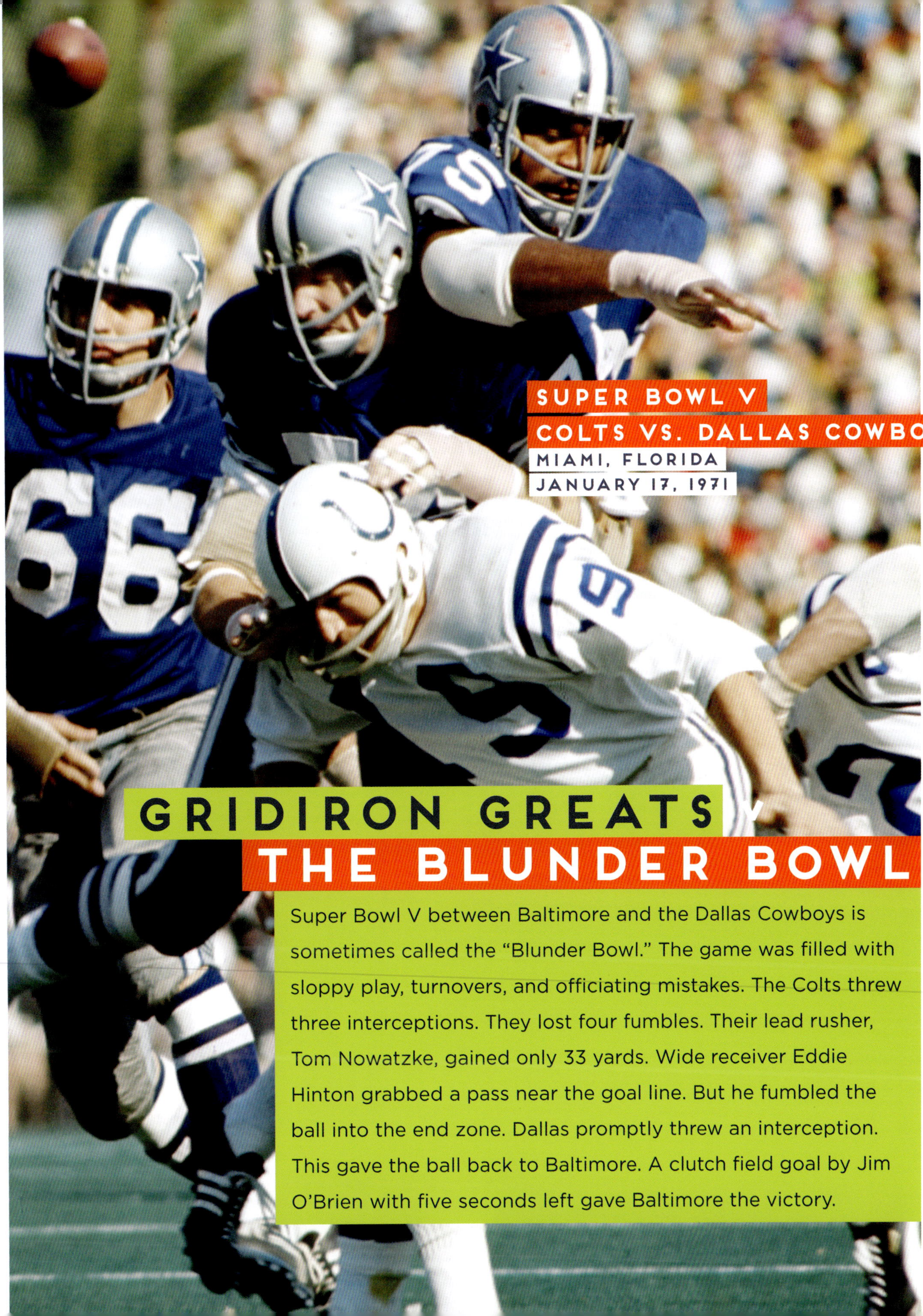

SUPER BOWL V
COLTS VS. DALLAS COWBOYS
MIAMI, FLORIDA
JANUARY 17, 1971

GRIDIRON GREATS
THE BLUNDER BOWL

Super Bowl V between Baltimore and the Dallas Cowboys is sometimes called the "Blunder Bowl." The game was filled with sloppy play, turnovers, and officiating mistakes. The Colts threw three interceptions. They lost four fumbles. Their lead rusher, Tom Nowatzke, gained only 33 yards. Wide receiver Eddie Hinton grabbed a pass near the goal line. But he fumbled the ball into the end zone. Dallas promptly threw an interception. This gave the ball back to Baltimore. A clutch field goal by Jim O'Brien with five seconds left gave Baltimore the victory.

SUPER BOWL V

In 1970, the AFL and NFL merged. The Colts cruised to 11–2–1. They enjoyed two playoff wins. Then they faced the Dallas Cowboys in Super Bowl V. Baltimore emerged with a narrow 16–13 win. The Colts made the playoffs again in 1971. But the Miami Dolphins pummeled them. Many of the great Colts players of the '60s were at the end of their careers. After a 5–9 finish in 1972, it was clear that the team needed new blood. Owner Robert Irsay traded Unitas to the San Diego Chargers. Johnny U left Baltimore as the NFL's all-time leader in pass completions (2,796), passing yards (39,768), and touchdown passes (287).

The Colts found their new quarterback in the 1973

BERT JONES

NFL Draft. Bert Jones stepped into the starting role two years later. He led the team to the playoffs for three years in a row. But the Colts lost in the divisional round each time. That set off a string of poor records. Baltimore won just two games in 1981. It finished with no wins in the strike-shortened 1982 season. The next year, Baltimore made John Elway the top overall draft pick. But he refused to play for the Colts.

LINEBACKER MIKE CURTIS

THE COLTS AT BALTIMORE'S MEMORIAL STADIUM

He thought they showed no promise. His agent said that Elway "would be a garbage collector before he'd play for Baltimore." The team had to trade him.

After the season, investors approached Irsay. They wanted him to move his team to Indianapolis. Irsay thought about the city's Hoosier Dome. It was a brand new 60,000-seat domed stadium. When Baltimore denied his plea for a new stadium, he decided to move.

QUARTERBACK PEYTON MANNING

MANNING TAKES THE REINS

Indiana fans embraced the team. Unfortunately, the Colts kept struggling. In 1987, they traded for star running back Eric Dickerson. He was known for his graceful yet hard-nosed style. Dickerson had already established himself as a top rusher with the Rams. He immediately helped the Colts improve to a 9–6 record. They took the American Football Conference (AFC) East Division title. They marched to their first playoff game in 10 years. But the Browns defeated them, 38–21. In 1988, Dickerson charged to a franchise-record 1,659 yards. The Colts went 9–7. They just barely missed the playoffs. Then the team crumbled. In 1991, it won just one game.

The Colts fought their way to 9–7 in 1992. But they slumped to 4–12 a year later. They added veteran quarterback Jim Harbaugh in 1994. He was known as "Captain Comeback." They also picked Marshall Faulk second overall in the

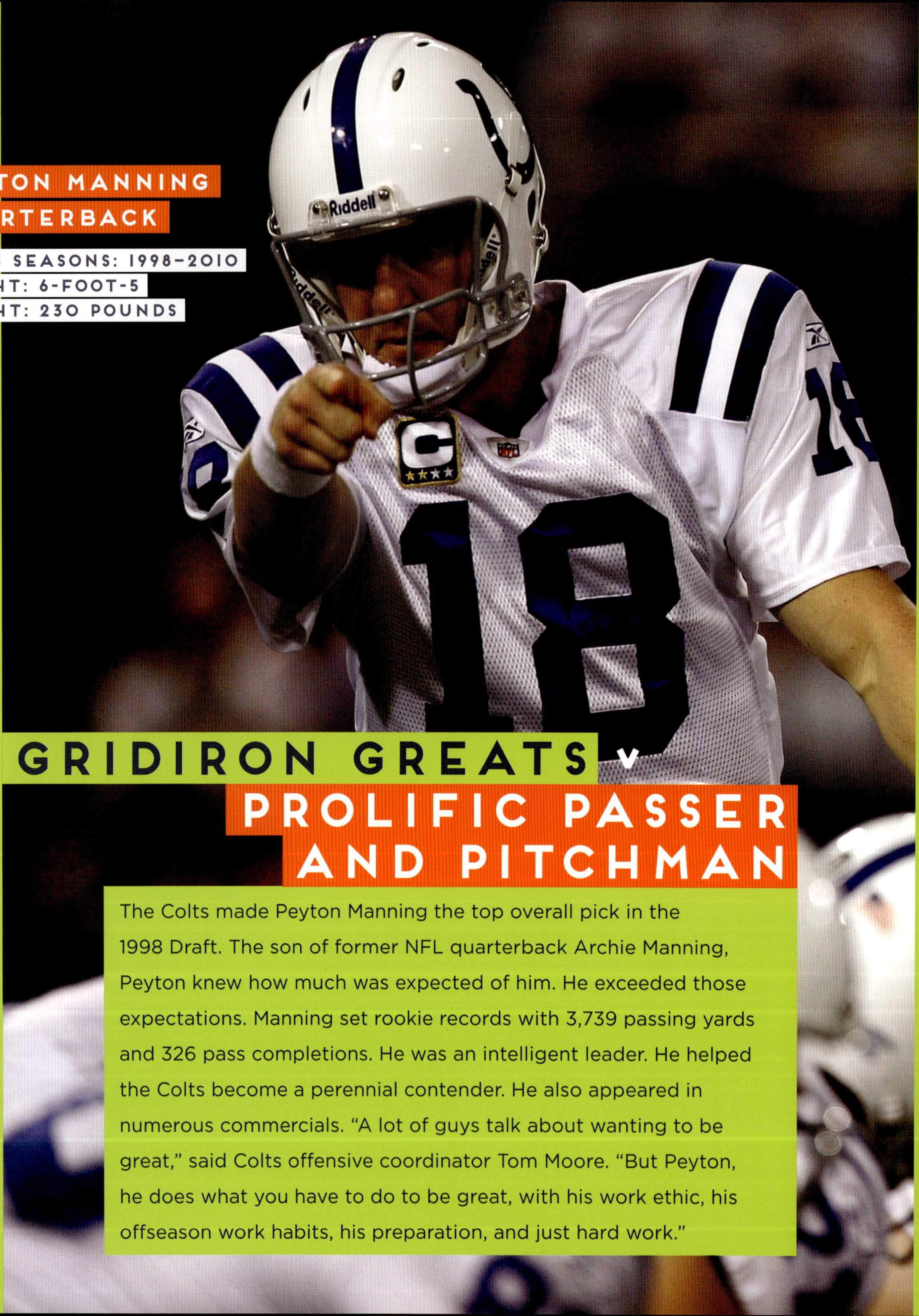

PEYTON MANNING
QUARTERBACK

COLTS SEASONS: 1998–2010
HEIGHT: 6-FOOT-5
WEIGHT: 230 POUNDS

GRIDIRON GREATS

PROLIFIC PASSER AND PITCHMAN

The Colts made Peyton Manning the top overall pick in the 1998 Draft. The son of former NFL quarterback Archie Manning, Peyton knew how much was expected of him. He exceeded those expectations. Manning set rookie records with 3,739 passing yards and 326 pass completions. He was an intelligent leader. He helped the Colts become a perennial contender. He also appeared in numerous commercials. “A lot of guys talk about wanting to be great,” said Colts offensive coordinator Tom Moore. “But Peyton, he does what you have to do to be great, with his work ethic, his offseason work habits, his preparation, and just hard work.”

266

266 GAMES PLAYED

539

539 CAREER PASSING TOUCHDOWNS

ERIC DICKERSON

Draft. The speedy running back was known for his shifty moves. In 1995, the Colts raced back to the postseason. After two playoff wins, the excitement came to an end. The Colts lost a 20–16 heartbreaker to the Pittsburgh Steelers in the AFC Championship Game. The powerful Steelers defeated them again in the 1996 playoffs.

The Colts slipped to 3–13 in 1997. This poor finish gave them the first overall pick in the 1998 Draft. They chose quarterback Peyton Manning. But Manning couldn't spur the Colts. Indianapolis again posted a 3–13 record. However, Manning showed signs of stardom. "He's the kind of guy who wants to be coached," said coach Jim Mora. "You can't overwork him. He's like a sponge."

In a startling turnaround, the Colts shot to 13–3 in 1999. They claimed the AFC East title for the first time since 1987. Manning, wide receiver Marvin Harrison, and running back Edgerrin James were one of the most feared offensive trios in the NFL. But the season came to a disappointing end. The Colts lost to the Tennessee Titans in the first round of the playoffs. Indianapolis returned to the playoffs in 2000. But Miami took the Wild Card game in overtime. The Colts slumped in 2001 but rebounded the next year. They were buoyed by additions such as defensive end Dwight Freeney. Unfortunately, the season ended on a bitter note. The Jets pounded Indianapolis, 41–0, in the playoffs. The Colts improved to 12–4 in 2003. But the New England Patriots defeated them in the AFC Championship Game.

In 2004, Manning threw a league-record 49 touchdown passes. He racked up 4,557 passing yards. He was named

Most Valuable Player (MVP). "It's difficult to pick one player out of the league and determine who is the most valuable," said coach Tony Dungy. "Peyton sets the tempo for us. We ask a lot of him and he's certainly delivered." Manning delivered a 12-win season. Indianapolis beat the Denver Broncos, 49–24, in the Wild Card. But the team was stifled by the Patriots a week later. The Colts improved to 14–2 in 2005. They suffered a narrow defeat at the hands of the Steelers in the playoffs.

MARSHALL FAULK

GRIDIRON GREATS

LOW PROFILE, HIGH PRODUCTIVITY

Today, wide receivers often perform outlandish, crowd-pleasing touchdown celebrations. But little was flashy about Marvin Harrison. He played smart and ran precise routes. He also caught lots of passes. He and Peyton Manning became one of the most successful "pitch-and-catch" tandems in NFL history. With just a look, they could switch plays at the line of scrimmage. Donovan McNabb, longtime quarterback for the Philadelphia Eagles, appreciated Harrison's style. "So many receivers go throughout their career talking about how great they are, and how much they're going to do. Marvin just does it," said McNabb.

MARVIN HARRISON
WIDE RECEIVER

COLTS SEASONS: 1996–2008
HEIGHT: 6 FEET
WEIGHT: 175 POUNDS

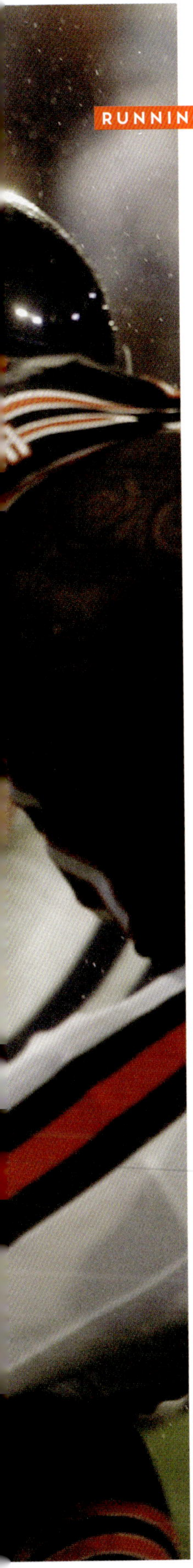

RUNNING BACK DEDE DORSEY

SUPER-BOWL BOUND

The Colts cruised to 12–4 in 2006. In the playoffs, they finally toppled the Patriots. This secured their place in Super Bowl XLI. They faced the Chicago Bears. The first half was plagued by sloppy play. Rain poured from the sky. The teams combined for six turnovers. In the second half, the Colts shook off the rain and the Bears. They won, 29–17. They finally brought home the Lombardi Trophy. Coach Dungy praised his team. "This may not be our best team in five years, but it was the closest and the most connected—and it showed in the way we played," he said.

Indianapolis maintained its momentum. It finished 13–3 and 12–4 the next two seasons. Both times, the team couldn't get past the

Chargers in the playoffs. In 2009, the Colts won their first 14 games. Fans hoped for an undefeated season. But coach Jim Caldwell pulled most of the starters in Week 16. He wanted them to rest for the postseason. The Colts lost that game and the final one. "The most important thing is to make certain that we are operating on all cylinders come the playoffs," explained Caldwell. "The most important season is the one coming up." His choice seemed to be correct. The Colts effortlessly won two playoff games. They reached Super Bowl XLIV against the New Orleans Saints. It was the Saints' first trip to a Super Bowl. Midway through the third quarter, the Colts were up by four. But then they stalled. New Orleans scored 18 unanswered points. The Saints won, 31–17.

The Colts' 10–6 record sent them to the playoffs for the ninth straight season in 2010. But they lost to the Jets by just one point in the Wild Card. After the season, Manning had surgery on his neck. He did not play during the 2011 season. Without him, the Colts won just two games.

The poor record gave Indianapolis the top pick in the 2012 Draft. It chose quarterback Andrew Luck. In each of his first three seasons, Luck led the Colts to an 11–5 mark. They reached the playoffs each time. In 2014, they advanced to the AFC Championship Game. There, they suffered an embarrassing 45–7 loss to the Patriots. The Colts went 8–8 in the next two seasons. After that, Luck

LEFT: TONY DUNGY AND RUNNING BACK DOMINIC RHODES

ANDREW LUCK

WIDE RECEIVER T. Y. HILTON

had surgery to correct a lingering shoulder injury. He missed the entire 2017 season. The following year, Luck returned. He threw for 4,593 yards and 39 touchdowns. The Colts raced into the postseason. But they could not overcome the Chiefs. Kansas City won the divisional round, 31–13.

History has taught the Colts that losing streaks don't last forever. The team boasts thrilling championship seasons as well as disappointing losses. Through it all, fans have supported their gridiron heroes. Fans and players alike are eager to expand the trophy case and add another championship soon.

TEAM STATS

NFL CHAMPIONSHIPS

1958, 1959, 1970, 2006

WEBSITES

INDIANAPOLIS COLTS

https://www.colts.com/

NFL: INDIANAPOLIS COLTS TEAM PAGE

http://www.nfl.com/teams/indianapoliscolts/profile?team=IND

INDEX

KICKER ADAM VINATIERI